DUNSTABLE DECADE
THE EIGHTIES
A collection of photographs

edited by Pat Lovering

To my Grandson
LEWIS
born 7.11.89
and the new generation of
Dunstablians of whom he is a
member.

Fig 1. The crossroads at the town centre, where the old Roman Watling Street crosses the ancient Icknield Way. *August 1989 (PL)*

First published March 1990
by
The Book Castle
12 Church Street
Dunstable
Bedfordshire LU5 4RU

© The Book Castle

ISBN 1 871199 35 2

Printed and bound by
White Crescent Press Ltd

Contents

Where possible, the date of each photograph is shown in italics to the right of the caption.
The source is indicated in parenthesis, together with the photographer, if known.

Publisher's Foreword

The Book Castle first opened its doors in February 1980, a new undertaking in a building dating back to 1872. Its aim was to present the riches of the book world to the widest possible public, and it is gratifying to look back and sense that the facility has been relished by so many customers, young and old.

I feel that a bookshop, though primarily a commercial undertaking, also has a special opportunity to act as one of the catalysts of local pride, knowledge and identity. Accordingly the mid-eighties saw the start of a local publishing venture under the Book Castle imprint. In looking for a way to mark the shop's first decade in the town, it seemed natural to commission a photographic selection that would both record the key events and capture something of the town's special character in the eighties. Dunstable is fortunate in being at once both small enough to feel personal and large enough to 'make things happen'.

The brief would have defeated a less able and conscientious editor than Pat Lovering, who has spent many hundreds of hours sifting through thousands of possible photographs and news stories. She has completed a formidable task in exemplary fashion, and I feel sure everyone in the town would wish me to thank her for providing us with this unique visual memory bank.

During the sixties and seventies Dunstable lost a number of historic buildings, though the eighties have been rather more conservation-minded. But who knows what the future may hold? Hopefully generations to come will also appreciate this pictorial glimpse into our present life-style. May it help to put flesh on their natural curiosity about their ancestors' environment and behaviour.

Paul Bowes

Fig 2. During the preparatory work for redecoration of the outside of the Book Castle in 1988 the original painted sign, marking the building's historic use as a drill hall, was temporarily uncovered above the doorway. Paul Bowes, the proprietor and publisher, stands outside.   *October 1988 (DG/JS)*

Foreword by the Mayor of Dunstable

Councillor K. S. Biswell

I am delighted to congratulate the Book Castle on the 10th Anniversary of their establishment in Dunstable. They have provided a valuable addition to the shopping facilities in our town and this publication is an excellent way of celebrating the Anniversary.

Dunstable is a rapidly developing town and the photographs in this publication provide a lasting reminder of the wide variety of community activities which have taken place over the last decade.

The Town Council have been pleased to be associated with this initiative.

Ken Biswell.

Kenneth S Biswell
Town Mayor of Dunstable

Fig 3. After its formation in 1985, Dunstable Town Council occupied The Friars in High Street South before moving to Grove House in High Street North in December 1989.   *August 1989 (PL)*

Fig 4. The Priory on New Year's Day 1982.   *January 1982 (CPA)*

Introduction

The Eighties – the national view

Looking back over the eighties, the decade takes shape as one of great contrasts and remarkable events.

Margaret Thatcher became the first woman Prime Minister, in June 1979, in a political system which has always been a largely male preserve. She then went on, in 1989, to become the longest serving Prime Minister in this century and the longest in continuous office since Lord Liverpool in the early part of the 19th century. It fell to her to lead the nation during the Falklands conflict, which with all the implications of any war overshadowed 1982.

Unemployment figures nationally rose alarmingly through the 2 million mark in 1980, to peak at 3.1 million in 1986(*1). In Dunstable, the effects of job losses and consequent loss of trade were very marked in the early part of the decade.

Great contrasts were evident in many areas: the stock market crashed spectacularly in 1987 after a long bullish period and recovered fitfully again over the following years. House prices which had been rising at an ever accelerating rate, peaked in 1988 and then fell by anything up to 20%.

In October 1984, a short news item brought the country's attention to the effects of a terrible famine and drought in Ethiopia: this proved to be the beginning of a great heightening of public awareness of Third World needs, triggering huge national and international fund-raising events to try to alleviate the effects of drought, famine, war and economic disasters.

There were a series of disasters in the areas of transport and of sport: a serious fire at Kings Cross underground station, the sinking of a cross-Channel ferry, plane and train crashes, a fire at the Bradford football stadium and the crushing of fans at Hillsborough.

Public awareness of the effects of pollution and the misuse of natural resources was also a feature of the latter part of the decade, with so-called "green" issues becoming politically important for the first time.

Two Royal weddings were celebrated loyally in Dunstable, as in every other town. Prince Charles married Lady Diana Spencer on July 29th 1981 and Prince Andrew married Sarah Ferguson on July 23rd 1986. The magnificence and pageantry of these occasions were made accessible to everyone by the television cameras.

The public shared in several other Royal events of note. The Prince and Princess of Wales had two sons: Prince William was born in June 1982 and Prince Harry in September 1984. The Duke and Duchess of York had a baby daughter, Princess Beatrice, born on the auspicious date of the eighth of August 1988. Princess Anne and Capt. Mark Phillips had a second child, their daughter Zara, in May 1981. Princess Anne, whose visits to Dunstable are pictured further on in this book, was accorded the title of Princess Royal in June 1988. Sadly, she and Capt. Phillips announced their separation in September 1989.

The weather, that great stalwart of national conversation, surpassed itself. In the Great Freeze of 1987, the lowest temperatures of the century were recorded: a temperature of minus 9.5 C was recorded at Luton (*2), and it was probably even lower in the more exposed parts of Dunstable. The gales in October 1987 were the worst for 300 years and changed the face of many parts of the country. Much snow fell in the winter of 1981/82, with a temperature of minus 8 deg C. recorded at Luton, and the heaviest rainfall of the decade in Dunstable, 49.5mm, was recorded on the 9th October 1987.

By contrast, the summer of 1989 was the sunniest this century. Actual temperatures did not reach those of 1976, but the hours of sunshine far exceeded it.

The Eighties – the Dunstable view

I asked several prominent Dunstablians for their view of the Dunstable of the eighties, and received many fascinating insights as a result.

Trevor Rix, the Chief Executive to the South Bedfordshire District Council considers that the 1980s will be remembered as the decade in which significant changes took place in Dunstable.

"In 1980", he writes, "the town was still heavily reliant upon the manufacturing industries which had supplied its main employment prospects since paper and printing companies became established at the end of the last century, followed by vehicle component manufacturers in the 1930s and truck assembly plants in the 1950s.

The closure of General Motors' truck assembly plant in 1986 threatened heavy job losses. Although the situation was saved by AWD Ltd. taking over the plant, the experience taught the town a lesson. It could no longer keep all its eggs in one basket.

The economic base of the town has become more diversified in recent years with the development of offices and modern industrial estates providing operations ranging from warehouse and distribution to computer companies.

The need to provide alternative wealth has led to a big drive to promote the town and the surrounding district as a tourist destination and, with this effort, has come a greater awareness of the environment and what needs to be done to preserve and enhance it."

Roger Vincett, Manager of Dunstable Recreation Centre during much of the decade, points out another aspect of the economic climate, however, when he writes, "The early 1980s were a time of redundancy and the beginning of a period of high unemployment but it can equally be said that 'the gloom and doom brought a leisure boom' as redundancy money and more free time saw a 20% growth in leisure pursuits.

Today's generally high socio-economic life style has resulted in high value property in the area, with high consumer spending. The most outstanding difference between 1980 and the present time is the growth of leisure time and the increase in the use of restaurants and the habit of eating out."

A generally high socio-economic life style does have its drawbacks, however. Mr Vincett goes on to report a local councillor at a District Council meeting remarking that "the costs for burials should be in line with the cost of living"!

David Madel, MP, has represented South (later South West) Bedfordshire in the House of Com- mons since 1970. "The most welcome change that has taken place in Dunstable in the last ten years is the fall in unemployment. This has been helped by Renault's acquisition of the old Chrysler plant, and by AWD taking over from General Motors at the plant opposite, thus ending the uncertainty over its future, both of which have done much to ensure our employment base in the truck industry.

We have also seen a widening of home ownership, partly through the sale of Council houses. Another development has been the establishment of a full Social Security office in Dunstable, so that people no longer have to travel to Luton to discuss their benefit problems.

The decade was also dominated by the threat to close Queensbury School and the eventually successful campaigns to keep it open. The event which means a great deal to so many of us in Dunstable was the reopening of Queensbury in September this year with Grant Maintained status."

Of course the question of an upper school closure also arose when I asked **David Fone,** OBE, BSc, FRGS, Head Teacher of Northfields Upper School, to give an overview of the decade from the point of view of education in the town. "The Comprehen-

Fig 5. Prince Michael of Kent visiting AWD Ltd, in Boscombe Road.   *March 1989 (DG)*

sive system of education on a three tier basis had been established by 1980,'' he writes. ''The decade has seen the consolidation and strengthening of Lower, Middle and Upper Schools.

In the Upper Schools, much of the decade has been dominated by the attempts to close an upper school – first Queensbury in 1982, then Houghton Regis and then Queensbury again in the face of falling school numbers.

The decade will be remembered for the large number of new initiatives which schools have been expected to implement – the GCE 'O' level and CSE examinations replaced by GCSE, the Technical and Vocational Education Initiative (TVEI), 'AS' Levels, the National Curriculum for all schools and Local Management of Schools which is with us as we turn into the next decade. All these, and many other initiatives have demanded much in-service training with a consequent quickening of the pace within the schools.

Technological advances have resulted in a vast increase in paperwork for head teachers and other staff.

Highlights of the decade must include our Golden Jubilee in 1986 and, for Manshead, their Cen-tenary celebration marking 100 years on two sites.''

I talked to **Steve Cook,** who has been an estate agent in the town since 1956, running his present business in Church Street since 1976, about the housing market in the last decade.

''The cost of a typical semi-detached house in the town in 1980 would be somewhere around £28,000,'' he told me, looking through his records. ''Now, in the present rather depressed market, you could expect to pay about £80,000 or £90,000. Prices rose in 1988 by about 10% up to August, and then fell back by about 20% to their present level.

I think that communications have changed Dunstable most: when I started in estate agency in 1956, this was a quiet market town where the community met together regularly at various events. The opening of the M1 and its increasing use altered the nature of the town, with people coming in from other areas and commuting regularly to London, Watford and so on, and to some extent this feeling of community was lost. Up to the early eighties the people to whom I sold houses were Dunstablians moving from one house to a bigger one, local youngsters buying their first house and so on. Most houses I sell these days are not sold to Dunstab-

Fig 6. Dr Keith Barker, the Headmaster, David Madel, MP, and the Chairman of the Governors Peter Roberts, opening Queensbury Upper School as a grant maintained school in September 1989.   *September 1989 (DG/JS)*

lians, but to people moving in to the town.

The biggest change in the town is, however, the amount of traffic." (All through this conversation, there was the steady thunder of vehicles passing immediately outside the shop, and this was during Dunstable's 'quiet' holiday weeks!) "In the early eighties it was at its heaviest in the mornings and evenings, but now it is incessant all through the day. If some solution isn't found, I think Dunstable will soon choke up altogether.

Of course the idea of a by-pass isn't new – when I started in 1956 the possibility appeared in Land Registry searches for the Borough Road/Great Northern Road/Station Road area even then.

At that time there were about five estate agents in the town, and we never thought that there would be more. What has changed the face of the business in the eighties, however, has been the influx of the multiples and institutions, and the rise of the 'yuppy' – a word I don't think we knew before 1980 – in so many areas like estate agency, investment, insurance, car sales, finance and so on."

One of Dunstable's most valuable institutions, celebrating its 125th anniversary in 1990, must be the Dunstable Gazette – always generous with its source materials and always knowledgeable concerning local affairs. **John Buckledee** is Editor of the Dunstable Gazette and Luton News. He was a reporter in Dunstable in the 1950s and was first made editor of the Dunstable Borough Gazette in 1964. He writes:

"The last ten years in Dunstable have seen a crucial change in attitude towards conservation.

Many of Dunstable's interesting houses and open spaces were destroyed in the sixties and seventies. There was little opposition at the time . . . there was a mania to tear down and begin anew, and those cautious souls who felt that the architects were running amok had no Prince Charles as their champion. The feeling then was that time would add charm to the new buildings . . . once the initial shock subsided.

The decade recorded in this book has seen increasing efforts to preserve what little is left in Dunstable and even to correct some of the smaller follies. The Windsock and the Quadrant clock have gone, unlamented, and the face of The Quadrant itself has been lifted. But there's not a lot that, inexpensively, can be done to Dunstable College or a score of other similar squat buildings, and every patch of surviving grass still needs guarding. The rugby field and, unbelievably, the Friary meadow are already under bricks and the cricket field will soon follow. There are even houses on the slopes of the Downs where the California dance hall and its swimming pool once lay. These newest estates are attractive in themselves – but the town now has too few green spaces.

It's ironic that the California, a gimcrack building constructed in the fifties around a huge wooden door rescued from a demolished stately home, is one modern building which is remembered now with real affection. At the time, it was hated by the town's establishment.

We on the Dunstable Gazette work week by week to record everything that is happening in the

Fig 7. All through the eighties the traffic continued to build up in Dunstable, bringing the town to a standstill on occasion with tailbacks the length of Dunstable's approach roads in September 1989. Here, the traffic in High Street South stretches back as far as the eye can see. Throughout the decade the debate surrounding the route of the proposed by-pass grew in intensity.   *August 1989 (CPA)*

town. It's fascinating for us to read this kind of retrospective volume and discover which of thousands of events are interesting to a later decade. Was there another Gary Cooper taking part in 1988's Grammar School centenary celebrations? We just hope that historians will find the face that they're seeking when they hunt through our microfilms in years to come."

In November 1988, Moore's, the drapery and clothing shop in High Street South, celebrated 80 years in the town. I asked **Pauline Keen,** whose grandparents founded the store and who was, in 1989, president of the Chamber of Commerce, how she saw the development of the decade.

"Probably for traders, the great improvement in the town has been the extensive improvements made to the shopping precinct in 1987. Up until this time there were many shabby units which gave Dunstable a very run down appearance. Quite a number of High Street giants moved in, which obviously helped to keep the consumer in Dunstable.

The minus side must be the large number of estate agents paying high prices for units. This unfortunately can mean that the individual shops are unable to run a viable business when property becomes so expensive. The increase in traffic has also had a detrimental effect on the traders; when the roads into the town are at a standstill, many shops find that there are far fewer shoppers around."

When I asked what she considered to be the most outstanding difference between 1980 and the present time, Mrs. Keen replied, "This must be the advent of the Dunstable Town Council who in a short time have promoted so many community activities in the town, and in many ways made the town a more attractive place." A sentiment expressed by a large number of people to whom I spoke.

I asked **Richard Walden,** the Town Clerk to Dunstable Town Council, for his overview of the decade.

"Dunstable has always had a strong sense of its separate identity and the town's history is full of incidents large and small showing how the townspeople have fought to preserve that identity.

For me, the story of the 1980s has been the re-establishment of a directly elected Dunstable Council. The early years of the decade were taken up with the struggle of South Bedfordshire District Council, all political parties, various interest groups and the inhabitants at large to persuade Central Government that there was a need for our own Council. They were, of course, successful and the Dunstable Town Council came onto the scene in April 1985.

Since then the Council have striven hard to promote a community spirit in the town and have instigated many initiatives which have become established dates in the town's calendar such as the Charity Fireworks, Christmas Street Decorations, Sunday afternoon Band Concerts, Orchestral Concerts and the Countryside Day etc.

The Council has also acted as the focal point for galvanising public opinion on a wide range of topics including preserving Queensbury School, reopening of the railway line, litter abatement and drug abuse. The increasing level of community activity in the town is reflected in the photographs in this book.

If asked for one anecdote to sum up the 1980s in Dunstable it would be this. Shortly after my appointment as Town Clerk to the Dunstable Town Council, my good friend and fellow Dunstable Football Club supporter Harold Stew, talked to me about the highly successful 1963 Dunstable Pageant of which he had been honorary secretary.

Harold reflected that such a major community event would doubtless be impossible to stage in present times.

Happily, he was proved wrong for the 1988

Fig 8. *The California Ballroom and swimming pool was demolished in January 1980, to make way for a housing estate. In the photograph can be seen the doors which originally came from a stately home. In the foreground is Chris Green, there to recover a time capsule buried by his father when the Ballroom was built in the fifties.*
January 1980 (LM/DG)

Dunstable Arts Festival proved to be the largest single community event ever held in the town. Over 2,000 people participated in the various concerts, exhibitions, displays and demonstrations held at venues throughout the town during the first two weeks of October. Attendances totalled well over 8,000, suggesting that the event touched the lives of over a quarter of the town's population.

Dunstable is indeed a town in which one can be proud to live and work."

The Eighties – a personal view

Looking through all the editions of the Dunstable Gazette for this period, one of the most striking characteristics of the eighties, for me, proved to be the volume and variety of charitable giving. Almost every event and even private parties seemed to be linked to the theme of "Yes, we're having a great time, but we haven't forgotten those less fortunate than ourselves," and I found this a most heartening attitude. Many of the organisations in the town which run social events are indeed formed entirely with the object of raising funds for charitable purposes, just as was, for example, the ancient Fraternity of St John the Baptist in the sixteenth century.

I noticed that the now ubiquitous oversized presentation cheque made its appearance in Dunstable in about 1983, but the date proved difficult to pin down exactly.

Compiling this glimpse into the eighties has been a remarkably interesting experience. My object has been to try to capture some of the events, scenes and people of the decade in photographs, to give the flavour of this bustling, historic town. It is inevitable, of course, that no matter how large the book, some photographs have to be left out from the wealth of material available. Other photographs prove impossible to track down, some prove unsuitable for reproduction, yet other events seem to have gone unrecorded. I hope that the photographs I have chosen provide a gentle nostalgic diversion for the Dunstablian reader as he recalls the events of the eighties, and that they help the newcomer to the town to appreciate the pleasures and treasures in store for him.

Pat Lovering

Footnotes: *1 Employment Intelligence Unit, Dept of Employment
*2 Ron Beard, Luton College. Philip Eden.

Fig 9. A Sunday afternoon band concert in the Priory Gardens.   *June 1988 (DTC/CPA)*

Fig 10. Harold Stew and Richard Walden look at some of the memorabilia of the Dunstable Pageant. The Pageant took place on June 24th–29th 1963 in the Priory Meadow, with a cast of over 1,000. Her Royal Highness the Duchess of Gloucester was present. The Pageant was to celebrate, in the words of the programme, "the great event of 1213" that is the consecration of the Priory Church of St Peter 750 years before, and "to remember with pride Queen Victoria's Charter of 1864". A film of the event, 100 colour slides, a sound recording and posters have been given to the Town Council, and a 25th anniversary exhibition was held in Dunstable Library in 1988. May 1987 (DG)

Fig 11. Chiltern Radio DJ Tony West, Immediate-Past President of Dunstable Lions Club Jack Bradley, and President Chris Banks give comedian Freddie Starr a cheque for the Home Farm Trust Appeal, raised by the Dunstable Lions Club through the Chiltern Radio "Radiothon". May 1988 (DLC)

Acknowledgements

I am greatly indebted to all the people in the town who have cheerfully lent me their photographs, answered my innumerable questions and checked the captions of countless pictures. The photographs are all acknowledged individually at the back of the book.

My sincere thanks go to Dunstable Town Council which has lent superb photographs for the book and encouraged the enterprise throughout and particularly to the Town Clerk, Richard Walden, who has helped immeasurably with his fund of local expertise.

In common with anyone who researches local history over the last 125 years, let alone the last 10, I have turned to the "Dunstable Gazette" for the day to day chronicles of the town. I would like to thank John Buckledee, the editor of the Dunstable Gazette and the Luton News, for his generous help and for the use of the photographic material in the Gazette's files.

The Gazette's photographic negatives for 1980/81 have been donated to the Luton Museum, and I would like to thank Stephen Bunker (Keeper of Local History) and Chris Grabham for their help in reproducing these.

Chiltern Photographic Arts have not only themselves provided many excellent photographs for this book, but have also done their usual first class work on most of the photoprocessing. Thank you.

There is a great deal of checking, ordering, indexing and numbering to be done in an enterprise of this nature; my thanks go to Ray Barlow for his meticulous help in this department, to Colin Bourne for his advice and to Trevor Wood for his expert and invaluable work in getting the book ready for printing.

Finally, this and many another local book would never have seen the light of day without the encouragement and talent of our publisher Paul Bowes. Thank you, Paul, and congratulations on the tenth birthday of The Book Castle.

PL

1980

Fig 12. Snow in Grove House Gardens, early in the year. *1980* (CPA)

Fig 13. High Street North, looking south, just before the Old Sugar Loaf. *January 1980* (CPA)

Fig 14. The Queensway Hall is the venue for many of the town's formal functions, such as the Mayor's Ball. It was opened in 1964 by the Lord Mayor of London, Sir James Harman. *1980* (CPA)

Fig 15. New Year's Day and the Christmas trees are still above the shop windows in High Street South. Buckles' men's outfitters is now Geoff Souster Menswear Ltd. Moore's can be seen on the left. *January 1980* (CPA)

Fig 16. A thatcher reridging the roof of the Norman King in Church Street. The Norman King is thought to stand on part of the site of Henry I's Royal residence in Dunstable. *February 1980* (LM/DG)

Fig 17. Dunstable Wanderers entered the Luton Town five-a-side tournament, which was televised. They are seen here with Kirk Stephens and a BBC crew cameraman preparing to appear in a sports programme.
February 1980 (LM/DG)

Fig 18. Grange Hill comes to Dunstable! Tucker (Todd Carty) and Cathy (Lyndy Brill), stars of BBC TV's most popular children's programme, meet a few of the hundreds of youngsters who queued to buy signed books on The Book Castle's first Saturday.
February 1980 (PB)

Fig 19. The London Gliding Club, on Dunstable Downs, celebrated its 50th anniversary in February. At the outbreak of war in 1939, Tim Hervey, pictured here, was the Club's first professional chief flying instructor and manager. During the war he was a prisoner of war, escaping twice from Germany and being involved in no less than eleven escape plots. The Gliding Club was itself a prisoner of war camp during the war years, housing Italian and German prisoners. During this period the tractor store was used as a jail. *March 1980* (LM/DG)

Fig 20. In this photograph Tim Hervey is in the repair shop at the Gliding Club. During the war it was the camp cookhouse. *March 1980* (LM/DG)

Fig 21. The prestigious Rotary Club award for services to the community went to Mrs Hope Pratt, former deputy head of Ashton St Peter Lower School and a leading figure among Church and secular organisations.
March 1980 (LM/DG)

Fig 22. Miss Clare Davis, the Dunstable Area Social Services Director, retired after 20 years in the town. The piper was Tony Spittle.
March 1980 (LM/DG)

Fig 23. The white lion carved on Dunstable Downs is a striking landmark in the area. It was carved 50 years ago for Whipsnade Zoo's opening and received a clean up in 1980 as part of the Golden Jubilee celebrations. Eight sailors from HMS Daedalus used 80 tons of whitener supplied by the Blue Circle Cement company, raking it all over the 6,500 square metres of the lion's figure. Here, his two forelegs have just been completed. *June 1980* (LM/DG)

Fig 24. Dr Erasmus Barlow, Secretary of the London Zoological Society, Blue Circle Assistant Advertising Manager Richard Wisdom, Public Relations man Barrie Hedges and the men from HMS Daedalus, positioning the "eye" on the lion. *June 1980* (LM/DG)

Fig 25. Manshead headmaster Mr L. P. Banfield MA, on his retirement in July 1980. He came to Dunstable in 1960 as headmaster of the old Grammar School. The local reorganisation of schools in 1971 meant that the Grammar School buildings were to house the present Ashton Middle School and Mr Banfield, his staff and pupils transferred to the present Manshead Upper School campus which was a purpose built Upper School. Mr Banfield was a Magistrate on the Ampthill Bench, and a founder member of the Dunstable Historical Society.   *July 1980* (LM/DG)

Fig 26. In July 1980, Mr David Madel, MP, celebrated ten years as Member of Parliament for South Bedfordshire. He is pictured here with his wife and family. Mr Madel was formerly a publishing executive.   *July 1980* (LM/DG)

Fig 27. The beginning of the Cross Paperware fire in High Street South in July 1980.   *July 1980* (CPA)

Fig 28. This was Dunstable's biggest fire, engaging 70 firemen and 12 tenders at its height.   *July 1980* (CPA)

Fig 29. The storage area went up in flames in a matter of minutes. The total damage was estimated at ¾ million pounds.
    July 1980 (CPA)

Fig 30. Brian Mathie and Peter Prior, the Parks Supervisor, admiring the Queen Mother's coat of arms, formed from 2,000 flowers. The display in High Street South was to celebrate the Queen Mother's 80th birthday and consisted of the Tudor crown, two rampant lions and shield adapted by Peter Prior for the purpose. *July 1980* (LM/DG)

Fig 31. The opening of Dunstable Town Cricket Club's new pavilion by Brian Taylor, the former Essex Captain, at the Bull Pond Lane ground. Also in the photograph can be seen Brian Chapman (Captain), Don Cutler (later President of the Club), Dick Barker, Cllr Bill Allen (Mayor of Dunstable), Reg Morgan (Chairman) and Arthur Buck (President). *May 1980* (LM/DG)

Fig 32. Brian Johnston, the broadcaster, and John Jeffries, Chief Flying Instructor at the London Gliding Club, recording the radio programme "Down Your Way" from Dunstable. *November 1980* (LM/DG)

Fig 33. The familiar local sight of a glider from the London Gliding Club being towed into the air. *1980* (LM/DG)

Fig 34. The empty vacancies board outside the Vauxhall Motors Ltd. Boscombe Road plant sums up the anxieties of the period as the plant went on to short-time working. 2-, 3- or 4-day weeks and redundancies were the order of the day. Vauxhall's shed 1,000 jobs at the beginning of 1981. *August 1980* (LM/DG)

1981

Fig 35. Detective Chief Inspector Selwyn Davies on his appointment as head of Dunstable CID. Mr Davies started on the beat in Bedfordshire in July 1958 and holds a long service and good conduct medal.
January 1981 (LM/DG)

Fig 36. Dunstable's Postmaster, Mr Arthur Way, retired after 43 years with the Post Office. *February 1981* (LM/DG)

Fig 37. Mrs Hilda Stevens, Mrs Rita Pugh, Mr Bernard Stevens and Mr Pat Pugh, at a presentation to mark the retirement of Mr Stevens as Chairman of Dunstable Magistrates. The presentation, made by the new Chairman Mr Pugh, also marked Mr. Stevens' 26 years on the Bench.
January 1981 (LM/DG)

Fig 38. Waterlow Ltd is Dunstable's largest printing works. Here the Waterlow Managing Director Brian Gurney is greeting Robert Maxwell who has arrived by helicopter. Mr Maxwell had invested £10 million into BPC (the owners of Waterlows), and subsequently promised to invest £1 million into the firm in 1981/2. *February 1981* (LM/DG)

Fig 39. Dunstable Teacher's Centre, in Chiltern Road, occupied the former Chiltern Road Infant School. It was threatened with closure in 1981, and subsequently became the Chiltern Radio station, retaining its appearance virtually intact. Here Hugh Garrod, head teacher of Totternhoe Lower School, is protesting against its closure. *February 1981* (LM/DG)

Fig 40. The Dunstable Carnival was organised by the Dunstable Round Table from 1976 to 1982. It was then organised each year by the Lions Club. It involves a procession of floats through the town, and an immense variety of novelty acts, displays, stalls and demonstrations at the Carnival site itself behind Kingsway. The proceeds from this huge event go to charity. 1981 had the dubious honour of being the muddiest carnival ever. However the "cowboys" in the photograph gamely carried on with their "fight to the death" even though they were more in danger of drowning in the mud than of dying from gunshot wounds!
May 1981 (LM/DG)

Fig 41. One of the Carnival floats passing the shops in Middle Row.   *May 1981* (GS)

Fig 42. The public valiantly lines the route by the Square, despite the weather.
May 1981 (GS)

Fig 43. Cllr Bill Allen, Mayor of Dunstable, adds his weight to the tug-of-war during the inter-services cadet tournament and display at Dunstable. The Dunstable Army Cadets won the Lionel Preston Cup.
June 1981 (LM/DG)

Fig 44. The 70 strong Concert Band from Dunstable Music School play for shoppers in the Quadrant.
July 1981 (LM/DG)

Fig 45. The 21st anniversary of The Dunstable Repertory Theatre Club, in the Little Theatre. In the front row of the photograph can be seen Jimmy Breed, Joyce Collins, Vic Tilley, Angela Goss, Richard Norris, Debbie Glen, Anne White and Eileen Diamond.
1981 (TDRTC)

Fig 46. The Rev Bruce Driver is pictured here outside the Vicarage in Friars Walk. Formerly a curate at the Priory Church he becomes the Priory's first Team Vicar with the formation of a Team Ministry for the Church of England Parish of Dunstable. The Team is headed by a Rector of Dunstable the Rev David Webb (previously Rector of the Priory) to oversee the three churches in the parish: St Augustine's, St Fremund's and the Priory Church of St Peter. Each church has its own Team Vicar and pastoral leadership.
July 1981 LM/DG)

Fig 47. Jennie Green and Gary Evans at the official opening of the Sewell Cutting Nature Reserve. The Nature Reserve, ¾ mile in length, is on the site of the old Dunstable to Leighton Buzzard railway line which was closed in 1962. The Naturalist Trust is to keep it free of encroaching scrub to encourage the plants and creatures which inhabit local grassland. *July 1981* (LM/DG)

Fig 48. Three apprentices from Waterlow's after the print trade's traditional "banging out" ceremony accorded at the end of their four year apprenticeship. Anything horrible from green ink to kitchen waste is poured over the hapless youngsters as they are wheeled round the factory in a trolley.
September 1981 (LM/DG)

28

Fig 49. These policemen are polishing up their boots in readiness to line the route to St Paul's for the wedding of Prince Charles and Lady Diana Spencer on July 29th. Pcs Laurence Hewitt, Graham Smith, Roger Wheeler, Martin Shaw and Graham Wharmby are preparing to be on duty at 6.45 am that morning. Sgt Bob Darts was on duty for the Royal Silver Jubilee Procession in 1977. "It is a great honour to be selected. We are all very proud to be going. A lot of other officers would have liked to have gone in our place," he said.   *July 1981* (LM/DG)

Fig 50. Barry Thomas, section supervisor at LuDun, the local workshops employing disabled people, with the wedding sampler sent to the Royal couple. It was commissioned by Mr Peter Holton, a Stevenage marketing consultant, and made at LuDun. It consists of the marriage vows worked in 100,000 silk stitches, with a rosewood frame. It was one of many gifts sent by individuals and companies in the area.

July 1981 (LM/DG)

Fig 51. A couple in fancy dress dancing at the Waterlow Road street party for the Royal wedding.   *July 1981* (LM/DG)

Fig 52. The Prince of Wales lit a wedding-eve beacon in Hyde Park on July 28th, which was echoed by 800 bonfires across the country. The Lord Lieutenant of Bedfordshire, Lt Col Hanmer Harbury, lit a bonfire 25′ high and 50′ in diameter on Dunstable Downs, watched by many local dignitaries and a large number of spectators.   *July 1981* (LM/DG)

Fig 53. The Cheveralls, on Oldhill Estate, held a street party for the Royal Wedding in which 80 children and residents took part. It included a barbecue, disco, tea party and games and was typical of street parties all over Dunstable.
July 1981 (LM/DG)

Fig 54. The children of St Christopher's Lower School made an imposing Royal backcloth for the occasion.
July 1981 (LM/DG)

Fig 55. 2000 people visited Dunstable Police Station on its open weekend in August. Here Baby Eleanor Jones meets police dog Bryn (with a certain degree of suspicion on both sides) and his handler PC Bob Newson.
August 1981 (LM/DG)

Fig 56. The rising crime rate prompted a return to the "Bobby on the beat" system as opposed to the use of police cars for patrolling. Pcs Graham Smith and Bob McGee explain the new moves to Mrs Elisabeth Taylor at St Mary's Gate opposite the Police Station.
October 1981 (LM/DG)

Fig 57. Princess Margaret presented Dunstable boy Robin Grant (front row, second right) with a cheque as winner of the painting competition organised by the NSPCC of which the Princess is President.
October 1981 (LM/DG)

Fig 58. Handbell ringers Gail Pemble, Jane Leach, Andrew Tournay, Lucy Shepherd, Alan Shepherd and Richard Horne play carols for the shoppers in Ashton Square. *December 1981* (LM/DG)

Fig. 59. A spell of Arctic conditions brings traffic to a standstill, and closes the schools. Business is brisk on the Downs, however, with a queue for tobogganing down the slopes. *December 1981* (LM/DG)

Fig 60. Snow fell in December of 1981, and January and February of 1982. In February a temperature of −8 deg C was recorded at Luton College of Higher Education. This photograph is of High Street South looking south, just before Lovers' Walk.
January 1982 (CPA)

Fig 61. Another view of High Street South, looking south, just before the Little Theatre. *January 1982* (CPA)

Fig 62. Dunstable market in the snow.
January 1982 (DG)

Fig 63. High Street South, looking
north. *January 1982* (CPA)

Fig 64. Princess Anne opening the new building and offices of ABC Travel Guides Ltd (now part of the Reed Travel Group) at the World Timetable Centre, Church Street, Dunstable.   *January 1982* (CEB)

Fig 65. In 1982 Dunstable Priory Church celebrated the 850th anniversary of its foundation. A project was launched to provide two hundred embroidered hassocks for the nave. This example, embroidered by Mrs Mabel Needham, shows the Priory Arms as designed by Worthington Smith, c1900.

August 1989 (JL/LW)

Fig 66. This hassock was embroidered by Miss Anne Baldock. It depicts John the Baptist between John Fayrey on his right and Mary, John Fayrey's wife, on his left. This design is based on the end panels of the Fayrey Pall, now on display in the Victoria and Albert Museum. The Fayrey Pall was given to the Fraternity of St John the Baptist, c1500, for use at members' funerals.   *August 1989* (JL/LW)

Fig 67. Dunstable Bowmen, here pictured at Dunstable Park Recreation Centre, where they meet.
February 1982 (DG)

Fig 68. President Elsie England and members of the Dunstable Business and Professional Women's Club at the Candle Ceremony. At this annual ceremony a candle is lit for every country where the Club exists. *March 1982* (DG)

Fig 69. Dunstable and District Flower Club is here celebrating its first anniversary in Dunstable Library. From left to right (standing) are: Phrena Wilkinson (Chairman), Shirley Hills, Anne Gilbert, Sue Williams, Barbara Prime. Seated: Penny Brown, Ann Peat and Rita Fleming.
April 1982 (DG)

Fig 70. Going out in style – Debbie Lindsey celebrates her last day of work as a single woman at Dunstable Library. Following library custom she has been dressed for the occasion by her friends and colleagues. Looking on are: front row Tina Fountain and Liz McGregor, back row Phil Sellars, Brenda Martin, Angela Kinchella, Jean Sands, Penny Smiles and Dorothy Garwood.   *March 1982* (DG)

Fig 71. Gary Alderson, Neil Emery, Stuart Matheson, and Andrea Caldecourt (seated), with the Marquis of Tavistock. The team came second in the Woburn Abbey Cup RNIB quiz at Manshead Upper School.
March 1982 (DG)

Fig 72. 166 hardy Dunstablians joining in the Dunstable Lions Club Fun Run. Here they are passing along High Street South, all helping to raise money for charity through sponsorship. *May 1982* (DG)

Fig 73. The Falklands conflict began in April 1982. In June, Johnnie Ritchie (in the bowler hat) and the staff of the Crown Inn in High Street North are celebrating victory in their usual exuberant way. *June 1982* (DG)

Fig 74. Chew's House, in High Street South, was built as a boys' charity school in 1715, and known as Chew's Grammar School. (PL)

Fig 75. A closer view of the inscription over the porch of Chew's House. William Chew died in 1712, without a wife or children. When his two sisters Mrs Frances Ashton and Mrs Jane Cart and his nephew Mr Thomas Aynscombe inherited his estate, they built the schoolhouse in his name. The Chews were one of the well-known charitable families in Dunstable.

(DTC/AH)

This School was erected and ENDOWED by Mʀˢ FRANCES ASHTON. Mʀˢ JANE CART and Mʀ THOMAS AYNSCOMBE. *Heirs at Law to* Wᴹ CHEW Esq. ANNO. DOM. 1715.

Fig 76. In order to increase the size of Chew's Grammar School, the Trustees bought the adjoining land and an extension to the school was begun in 1883. This building is now the Little Theatre.
(DTC)

Fig 77. The Matchmaker was The Dunstable Repertory Theatre Club's 150th production. Shown in this photograph are Angela Goss, Ian Hamilton-Smith, Anne White and Mark Cook.
January 1982 (TDRTC)

Fig 78. Richard Norris stood down after 22 years as chairman of The Dunstable Repertory Theatre Club. He had seen the club change from a small acting company staging plays in the old Town Hall, to a group with 1,000 members, their own theatre and a Young Rep for up and coming youngsters. He is pictured here inside the Little Theatre in High Street South.
July 1982 (DG/TDRTC)

Fig 79. Flooding occurs quite frequently in Church Street. Here the water is lying in the forecourt of Priory Hall.
June 1982 (GS)

Fig 80. And across the road, the water lies in front of Ashton St Peter Lower School.   *June 1982* (GS)

Fig 81. The Saracen's Head in High Street South is Dunstable's oldest surviving inn, dating from the 16th century. As a consequence, it lies well below the present day street level. Here, the fire brigade are busy pumping out the flood water.
June 1982 (CPA)

Fig 82. For some householders in Stipers Hill it was "all hands to the buckets". *June 1982* (CPA)

Fig. 83. And at the top of Church Street, police have closed the road and redirected the traffic. *June 1982* (CPA)

Fig 84. The Priory Church Choir "terrifying" the neighbourhood on their Carnival float. *May 1982* (GS)

Fig 85. Roland Dodge appeals for a catch in the LuDun Cup Final. Dunstable Town Cricket Club won the trophy for the first time in a decade. *July 1982* (DG)

Fig 86. The Dunstable Jobcentre with Bob Morgan, the manager, outside. Bob retired in 1989 after many years in this senior position despite severe physical handicap. Unemployment peaked in Dunstable in August 1982 at 4,032. In July 1989 it had fallen to 787.*
August 1982 (DG)

*Employment Intelligence Unit, Department of Employment.

Fig 87. Vincent Comb received injuries from machine-gun fire in the push to take Port Stanley in the Falklands. Here he is attending a civic reception in his honour. He is pictured with the Mayor, Cllr Stuart Brett and his wife Doris.
August 1982 (DG)

Fig 88. Another local hero Mick Stanton was in the Merchant Navy, on the hospital ship Uganda. He is pictured here, on his return from the Falklands, with his parents and two sisters.
August 1982 (DG)

1983

Fig 89. In September of 1981, the Priory bells fell silent for the first time in 206 years. The old bell frame was in danger of collapse. It had been carrying eight bells on a frame designed to carry five, since 1776. Here seven of the eight bells are being transported back to Whitechapel Bell Foundry to be adapted for the new frame being built. *January 1983* (DG)

Fig 90. At the end of January, the wearing of seat belts in the front seats of cars became compulsory. WPc Karen Page is demonstrating the new law.
February 1983 (DG)

Fig 91. The Delco Products Judo Club is admiring its many trophies after a particularly successful year.
January 1983 (DG)

Fig 92. Lance Percival, the television personality, celebrating with Dunstable Round Table the 30th anniversary of their charter. In the photograph are: front row Graham Smith (Chairman, Area 42 Round Table), Lance Percival, Neil Munro (Immediate Past Chairman, Dunstable Round Table). Second row Colonel Cy Goff (USAF Chicksands, Commanding Officer). Third row Dennis Wilkins, (Chairman, Dunstable 41 Club), Robert Tigg (Chairman, Dunstable Round Table). Back row Dennis Tizzard (Honorary Secretary, Round Table British Isles).   *September 1983* (DG)

Fig 93. In May, the inaugural dinner took place of the Rotary Club of Dunstable Downs. In this photograph were: Front row Derrick Hood, Peter Green (the Rotary Club of Dunstable representative who formulated the Club), the Rotary District 109 Extension Officer Don Sawyer, Neil Munro, Brian Carter, Roger Camp; second row Mike Chapple, John Stevens, Alan Turvey, Dudley Lowe, Philip Johnson, Michael Hicks, Eric Bradshaw, David Turner, Dick Robinson; third row Jim Page, Derek Bird, Peter Horstman, John Dent, Brian O'Hara, Robert Doody, Paul Rossi, Clifford Bygrave, Alistair Lockhart.   *May 1983* (DDRC)

Fig 94. Cllr Mrs Mary Biswell, Chairman of South Bedfordshire District Council, Mr Ken Biswell, and Roy Wilson, the Chairman's Officer, getting into the official car. Cllr Mrs Biswell remarked that using the car for official business would make a change for her – being a non-driver, she usually travelled by bus.   *June 1983* (DG)

Fig 95. The Dunstable WRVS meals on wheels team joined Leighton Buzzard WRVS members to practise their emergency food preparation skills in the open. The photograph includes Mrs Dol Brownlie, Mrs Anne Rowe and Mr Gerald Glover.   *August 1983* (DG/WRVS)

Fig 96. The 3rd Battalion of the Royal Anglian Regiment exercising its right of freedom to parade through the town. The salute is being taken in High Street South by the Mayor Cllr Jim McAllister and Major General Anthony Ward Booth, Deputy Colonel of the regiment. *July 1983* (DG)

Fig 97. An interested section of the crowd lining the route of the parade. The two young spectators on the right are obviously ready to augment the percussion section of the band. *July 1983* (DG)

Fig 98. Prince Michael of Kent, President of the Institute of Motor Industries, visits Henly's as part of a fact-finding mission. He is seen speaking to Henly's general manager John Connelly.   *May 1983* (DG)

Fig 99. After exercising their rights of Freedom of Entry to parade through the town "with bayonets fixed, drums beating and colours flying" Mayor Cllr Jim McAllister inspects the volunteer 201 Field Battery, Royal Artillery, The Beds and Herts Yeomanry, in the Queensway car park.   *October 1983* (DG)

Fig 100. An unusual panoramic view westwards from the Priory tower. In the left hand foreground can be seen the War Memorial, with the Priory Gardens in the middle distance and the back of Priory House. Slightly to the right is the spire of the Methodist Church in the Square. To the right of centre is Eastgate House and beyond that number 4 High Street North. Slightly to the left can be seen the West Street New Covenant Church. The Quadrant is to the right of the picture, with the tall Quadrant House building extreme right.

October 1983 (OR)

Fig 101. Dunstable Town Bowling Club celebrates its 75th anniversary. The Club moved to its present home in Hawthorn Close in 1971. It was previously located at the end of Nicholas Lane behind Ashton Lower School. *June 1983* (DG)

Fig. 102. Brian Willoughby and Northfields School Band. In the front is vocalist Vicky Moon. The Band was and is entirely self-financing. In 1983 it financed a Rhineland tour and was looking forward to a tour of Austria. *November 1983* (DG)

Fig 103. Princess Anne visiting the Queensway Hall, accompanied by Cllr Mrs Mary Biswell, Chairman of South Bedfordshire District Council. *April 1984* (DG)

Fig 104. Dunstable Downs Golf Club in its spectacular setting on the Downs above the town. *undated* (DTC/BT)

Fig 105. The Rev David Self, with his wife Carol and their Rhodesian Ridgeback, Ailsa, pictured at home in the Rectory in Furness Avenue. David became the new Rector of the Parish in September. *1984* (DS)

Fig 106. Omer Roucoux at work on the manuscript of "The Roman Watling Street" published by the Dunstable Museum Trust in 1984. *May 1984* (OR)

Fig 107. Local butcher and Justice of the Peace Mike Tilley finds himself behind bars in a good cause. Natalie Sear and Lisa Strange provide him with a nice cup of tea during the National Brownie Guide Tea Making Fortnight. *May 1984* (DG)

Fig 108. Horace Game came to Dunstable in the nineteen fifties and is here celebrating 25 years' service with South Bedfordshire District Council. He received a television and a microwave cooker.   *May 1984* (DG)

Fig 109. An appropriate photograph of the cast of The Dunstable Repertory Theatre Club's production of "Outside Edge". Included are Mark Cook, Janet McClurg, David Brooker, and Barbara Morton.   *May 1984* (DG/TDRTC)

Fig 110. On the 50th anniversary of Delco's arrival in Dunstable, South West Bedfordshire's MP David Madel is looking at the eighties' style equipment in use. *June 1984* (DG)

Fig 111. When the arrival of the AC Sphinx Sparking Plug Company was announced in January 1934, the headline in the Dunstable Borough Gazette read, "Adjunct to Dunstable's Architectural Wealth" and the front page article went on to say that the building would "enhance the architectural beauty of the town and create a favourable impression upon travellers who pass through the borough." It received an enthusiastic welcome all round. During the War, the factory made spark plugs for the giant Flying Fortresses and other service machines. This is a modern photograph of the building. *August 1989* (PL)

Fig 112. The staff of Marks and Spencer Distribution Centre donate a Vauxhall Astra estate car to Dunstable Red Cross. The donation included a contribution from Marks and Spencer as part of its Centenary Year effort. The car is to be used for transporting the elderly and the handicapped and other Red Cross work in the area. Here the Distribution Centre Manager Michael Brazeley hands over the keys to Dunstable central organiser Mrs. Winifred Whitten.
June 1984 (DG)

Fig 113. Jane Steer wins the first George Curran trophy for endeavour and David Brooker wins an award from the Mid Anglian Engineering Employers' Association. Both awards were made by the Dunstable England footballer Kerry Dixon at Dunstable College. George Curran, donor of the trophy and former Principal of the College, died in August 1984.
July 1984 (DG)

Fig 114. The enraptured Punch and Judy audience at Ashton St Peter Lower School's Strawberry Fair.
June 1984 (GS)

Fig 115. Ashton St Peter Lower School, Church Street. (GS)

Fig 116. Playschemes are operated all over Dunstable during the summer holidays. These children are enjoying themselves at Hadrian Lower School.   *August 1984* (DG)

Fig 117. "Darkie" (real name Amos Cameron), sold newspapers in Dunstable town centre for 40 years in the middle of High Street North, often amidst the traffic, until he took delivery of a little kiosk put up outside the Nag's Head in the sixties. He is wearing a sombrero given to him by a local cafe proprietor after her summer holiday. He stopped selling newspapers in 1985, because of ill health, and died aged 89 in January 1986.   *August 1984* (DG)

Fig 118. The annual "Statty" or Statute Fair in the Queensway Hall car park. The fair has ancient origins and was for the hiring of servants and farm labourers, although today it is simply a fun fair. It used to be held in The Square, but was moved in the sixties. *August 1984* (DG)

Fig 119. The Rev George Simons, the new Methodist Minister in Dunstable, with his wife, in front of the Methodist Church in The Square. Mr Simons retired in 1989.   *October 1984* (DG)

Fig 120. The London Gliding Club introduced flights for the disabled in the Year of the Disabled, 1981. Colin Cruse is in one of the gliders with a member of Dunstable and District Handicapped Persons Typing Club. On this occasion the flights were paid for by the proceeds of a charity cricket match and donations.
August 1984 (DG)

Fig 121. Miss Christina Scott retired as head teacher of Queensbury Upper School after 40 years as a teacher and 25 years as a head. When she took over the school, it was still being built; she chose the name Queen Eleanor's School for Girls. In the 1971 reorganisation of schools in Dunstable, Queen Eleanor's amalgamated with Kingsbury Technical School and became Queensbury Upper School.
December 1984 (DG)

Fig 122. Ken Ball, the local auctioneer, with Michelle Holt at a charity auction.
December 1984 (DG)

1985

Fig 123. The Marquis of Tavistock with Rafael Blanco, Andrew Wallis, Emma Mahn (holding a 140 year old spade) and Stephen Mills, voluntary assistant Youth Leader, at Woburn Abbey. They had been planting Wilbury Youth Club's oak tree to symbolise the start of International Youth Year in Bedfordshire.
January 1985 (DG)

Fig 124. Sledging on the Downs is as popular as ever. The dog evidently preferred its usual method of getting down the slopes.
January 1985 (DG)

Fig 125. Three visitors from Dunstable, Massachusetts, in the USA, which has a population of only 2,000. They are Charlotte Pogue, a data processing manager, Susan Psadakis, a teacher and Lucy Kennedy, an historian.
May 1985 (DG)

Fig 126. The closure of the Priory Hospital for elderly people was announced; the Department was to move to St Mary's, Luton.
January 1985 (DG)

Fig 127 The annual procession of witness on Good Friday, organised by the local Council of Churches, outside the Priory. Christians march through the town, stopping for readings and hymns.   *April 1985* (LE)

Fig 128. The Good Friday procession walking along High Street North.   *April 1985* (LE)

Fig 129. During the 19th century, The Crown Inn was called The Crow. Its name was changed to the Crown Inn in 1870. It may also have been a beer house called The Raven in the 17th century, *1985* (LE)

Fig 130. Harold Stew with Directors, Officials, helpers and friends assembled for the Club Dinner given in his honour on his retirement as Dunstable Football Club Secretary. Harold had been variously Secretary, Company Secretary and Director of the Club since its inception in 1950. In those days, the Club played on ground leased from Gerald Bagshawe at Kingsway (where The Mall now stands). The Club moved to its present site off Brewers Hill Road, and in 1962 Walter Creasey (after whom the Club's ground is named) formed a company to improve the standard of football in the town. George Best and Jeff Astle have played with the team, and they have played friendly matches against first division teams such as Aston Villa, Chelsea and Manchester United, whom they beat 3–2! The team plays in the Southern League and has represented the town in places as far apart as Shrewsbury and Devon. *1985* (DFC)

Fig 131. Mrs Christine Gerrard and her guide dog Gail. As well as being an accomplished musician, Mrs Gerrard is well known locally for her work raising funds for Guide Dogs for the Blind and Enterprises by the Blind.
August 1985 (DG)

Fig 132. Charlie Cole's Cycle Shop in High Street North was a listed 16th century building. The conservation specialist Philip Carstairs and his assistant are lifting 16th/17th century wall paintings, discovered behind a wooden partition, from the wall ready for their preservation. *June 1985* (DG)

Fig 133. The Norman King and Old Palace Lodge Hotel in Church Street. *1985* (DTC/OR)

Fig 134. The Saracen's Head in High Street South was formerly the Priory Hospice and later a coaching inn. It is Dunstable's oldest surviving inn. *1985* (DTC/AH)

Fig 135. Queen Eleanor's statue in the newly-opened Eleanor's Cross shopping precinct (running from High Street North to Albion Street). The statue is in bronze and was sculpted by Dora Barrett. It measures more than seven feet high, and weighs nearly one ton. *1985* (DTC/OR)

Fig 136. Richard Norris and Chairman Jimmy Breed at the refurbished Little Theatre in High Street South. Plush raked seats were installed, plus new carpeting and a centre aisle.
Sept. 1985 (DG)

Fig 137. Gurney Burgess, Press Officer for the Royal British Legion, on the scaffolding at Robinson and White's site at Dickins Yard off Burr Street, selling poppies to two young construction workers.   *November 1985* (DG)

Fig 138. The Victorian pub, appropriately named the Victoria, in West Street.   *1985* (DTC/CPA)

Fig 139. A presentation of tapes and video to the Children's Ward of the Luton and Dunstable Hospital. In the photograph are the President of the Inner Wheel Club of Dunstable, Lorraine Stott, and the President of the Rotary Club of Dunstable, Colin Bourne, together with hospital staff and children. *August 1985* (CEB)

Fig 140. Dunstable Amateur Operatic Society's production of Bizet's "Carmen" in the Queensway Hall, which marked their 21st birthday. *October 1985* (PG)

Fig 141. Some of the past Mayors of Dunstable:
Back row, left to right:
Mr. H.W. Parrott – 1962/3, Mr E.S. Clark – 1974/5, Mr P.J. Newton, JP – 1978/9 and 1981/2, Mr W.B. Rycroft 1977/8, Mr R. Wyles 1969/70, Mr C.G. Clark 1979/80
Front row, left to right:
Mr S.J.G. Molyneaux, JP – 1976/7, Mr J. Palmer – 1959/61, Mr N.P. Goodman – 1985/6, Mrs E.D. Poulmell 1975/6, Mr L.C. Worby – 1964/5.   *1985* (DTC)

Fig 142. Dunstable Town Council which was formed in April 1985, moved to its new premises The Friars in High Street South. There was an opening celebration in December, at which Jennifer, the Town Mayor Nick Goodman's daughter, is pictured switching on the lights of the Christmas tree outside the building.   *December 1985* (DG)

Fig 143. The Priory muffled in snow. *1986* (BE)

Fig 144. The Anchor Gateway (the refurbished rounded arch in this photograph) was the entrance to a 16th century inn, now demolished. The Anchor Inn (now the Halifax Building Society branch) was built on its site, but the old gateway was retained. *1986* (DTC)

Fig 145. Nigel Benson is presenting the Mayor Cllr Nick Goodman with framed prints from his book Dunstable in Detail which was published by The Book Castle in November 1986.
May 1986 (DG)

Fig 146. Vivienne Evans presenting the Mayor of Dunstable Cllr Nick Goodman and the Mayor of Houghton Regis Cllr Jim Pergunas with a copy of her recently published work The Book of Dunstable and Houghton Regis, in Dunstable Library.
January 1986 (VE/T)

Fig 147. The opening at The Friars of the Museum Trust's History and Arts Week, which coincided with the anniversary of the forming of the Trust. The Week included a display of the robes and insignia of office, a town trail, a travelling exhibition of the history and growth of Dunstable, guided tours of the Priory and many other attractions. The Mayor, Cllr Nick Goodman, is showing the Mace to an appreciative audience. On the left is the Chairman of the Trust David Hornsby, Ron Grace, the Publicity Officer Vaughan Basham, the Secretary Mrs Janet Webb, Alan Fisher and the Treasurer Barry Horne.
May 1986 (DG)

Fig 148. The Hospice at Home Volunteers and other charities benefited from a charity ball at the Queensway Hall organised by the Inner Wheel and Rotary Clubs. In the photograph are Dunstable Rotary Club president Colin Bourne and his wife Joy and Inner Wheel President Lorraine Stott and her husband Bev (Rotary Club President 1988/9). *January 1986* (CEB)

Fig 149. Bruce Turvey, well-known photographer in Dunstable for over 30 years, at his exhibition "Captured Moments" in Dunstable Library, part of the Museum Trust's History and Art Week. *March 1986* (DG)

Fig 150. Manshead Upper School's "Youth Speaks" team (Samantha Jenner, Stuart Burrows and Stephen Murch) became the first senior Dunstable school team to win through to the grand regional finals of the annual Dunstable Rotary Club Youth Speaks contest. In addition the fourth form all-girl team of Emma Bowes, Emma Bowley and Sally Wood won the Bedfordshire "Read Out" Competition. This was a county-wide verse speaking competition in which 40 schools took part. In the photograph are shown front row: Sally Wood, Emma Bowes and Emma Bowley and in the back row Stephen Murch, Samantha Jenner and Stuart Burrows. *March 1986* (DG/PB)

Fig 151. The World Trampoline Champion Andrea Holmes in training at Dunstable Park Recreation Centre. *1986* (DTC/AH)

Fig 152. Northfields Senior Mixed School (now Northfields Upper School) opened on the 15th January 1936. The Dunstable Borough Gazette called it "a monument to the advance of education." It was built for the children of workers at the AC Sphinx Sparking Plug Company. The Chairman of Governors, Mr E. Patterson, plants a tree to mark the Jubilee watched by pupils of the school and the headmaster, Mr Fone.
March 1986 (DG/NS)

Fig 153. In this photograph David Fone OBE (Headmaster from 1968), Fred Langley (Headmaster from 1958–63) and Kenneth Keates (1947–1980, Second Master 1961–80) look at Mr Keates' book on the history of the school, produced to mark its Golden Jubilee. Mr Keates died in 1988.
May 1986 (DG/NS)

Fig 154. The annual Keep Fit Rally of the Bedfordshire Branch of the Eastern Counties Keep Fit Association takes place in the Queensway Hall. There are classes from Queensbury Upper School (3), Watling School, Delco Products, and Northfields Further Education class included in this photograph.
March 1986 (DG)

Fig 155. The Dunstable Cowboys American Football team meet the Dallas Cowboys star Ed "Too Tall" Jones in Hyde Park. Ed is 6'9" tall and weighs 287 lbs.   *June 1986* (DG)

Fig 156. Cmdr David Brice RN inspects the Dunstable Sea Cadets and awards a burgee for high achievement. The Sea Cadets meet in the Old Mill, which can be seen in the background. The Mill was built in 1839 and was commissioned as the "Training Ship Lionel Preston" in 1948.   *June 1986* (DG)

Fig 157. The old Post Office was purpose built in 1912 and was in use as a post office and later as a sorting office until 1984. In 1986 the rear of the building was demolished, leaving only the facade standing. The front of the building is shown here. *1986* (VB)

Fig 158. At the back of the old Post Office building nothing was left standing at this stage of reconstruction except the front wall. *1986* (BE)

Fig 160. Manager Tom Waring (right) and staff in front of the mural found hidden behind a partitioned wall in the premises now occupied by the Nationwide Anglia offices. The mural is permanently displayed to the public in the main Banking Hall. It is thought to depict a hunting scene and to date from the 16th/17th centuries. The building itself contains original 16th century beam work. *October 1986* (DG)

Fig 159. In July 1988, the DHSS moved into the completely reconstructed building. This photograph shows the present day offices from High Street North. *August 1989* (PL)

Fig 161. The staff of Moore's in High Street South celebrating the wedding of Prince Andrew and Sarah Ferguson on July 23rd.
July 1986 (DG)

Fig 162. The Dunstable Football Club 1986/87 team. Dunstable Town, as they are usually called, won the Bedfordshire County Senior Cup four times in a row, in 1985/6, 1986/7, 1987/8 and 1988/9, something which had never been done before.
1986 (DFC)

Fig 163. Dunstable Town under 11 team for 1986/7, the Junior Blues, with a representative of Waterlow Ltd, and John Crumley, the Football Club Secretary. The Town expanded to run four Junior Blues teams in the 1989/90 season, from under 11s to under 14s.   *1986* (DFC)

Fig 164. The interior of St Mary's Roman Catholic Church in West Street. The church celebrated its Silver Jubilee in May 1989.
August 1986 (DG)

Fig 165. Canon Edward Charles was Rector of Dunstable from 1966–1973. He is seen here celebrating the 50th anniversary of his ordination with some of the clergy who were with him at that time. The photograph shows Canon Charles on the left, Priory Vicar Rev Bruce Driver (who was formerly curate at the Priory), Mrs Ruth Charles, Rev David Bracey, (formerly curate at St Augustine's) and Rev Robert Nokes, (also formerly curate at the Priory). *June 1986* (LE)

Fig 166. The inauguration of the South Beds Dial-a-Ride transport service for the disabled. Front row, third from the left is Bob Mumford the organiser of South Beds Dial-a-Ride, behind the wheelchair on the left is Cllr Bil Musannif Mayor of Dunstable, beside him to the right is Cllr E.R. Bartley the Deputy Mayor of Houghton Regis, in the wheelchair to the right is Bob Morgan Chairman of South Beds Dial-a-Ride, to his right Cllr Harland Rees Chairman of South Beds District Council and Cllr Mrs Marion McCarroll Mayor of Luton. The organisation went on to operate four minibuses from its headquarters in Winfield Street in 1989.

September 1986 (JS)

Fig. 167. 21 Dunstable firemen and their colleagues from Wembley triumphant after completing a gruelling Wembley to Dunstable ladder push for charity. They covered 40 miles in 8 hrs, pushing a ¾ ton ladder.

August 1986 (DG)

Fig 168. Past and present members of Dunstable Youth Hostels Association celebrating the group's 21st Anniversary.

September 1986. (DG)

Fig 169. The County Library and the County Offices in Vernon Place.   *1986* (DTC)

Fig 170. The Dunstable Magistrates Court in Court Drive.   *1986* (DTC)

Fig 171. Church Street, looking east. On the right is the Priory graveyard. On the left, the roofs of the doctors' surgery, Kingsbury House (formerly the farm house of Kingsbury Farm), The Old Palace Lodge, the thatched roof of The Norman King (all these last three believed to be on the site of Henry 1's Royal residence in Dunstable) and the white walls and roof of the Ladies Lodge Almshouses built between 1740–43. In the distance can be seen the railway bridge. *November 1986* (GS)

Fig 172. This panoramic view of the northern part of the town shows the Queensway Hall on the left, Dunstable Park Recreation Centre just right of centre and Dunstable College. *November 1986* (GS)

Fig 173. The pupils at Brewers Hill celebrating their Harvest Festival. 40 residents from sheltered accommodation in Croft Green and Saxon Close were treated to a meal which the fourth year pupils funded, cooked and served. The second year pupils entertained them with songs and sketches. The youngest pupils held a traditional harvest festival service and the produce they collected was made up into parcels and distributed to local OAPs by the third year pupils. *October 1986* (DG)

Fig 174. Dunstable Ladies Choir enjoying a joke on his birthday with Frank Ifield, the singer, outside his home at Whipsnade. Marie Westley their conductor is on the right, and Pat Lovering is on the left. *November 1986* (JS)

Fig 175. Miss Sybil Bate retired from Icknield Lower School after 18 years as Head Teacher.
December 1986 (DG)

Fig 176. The Dunstable Swimming Club's Christmas Synchro Display team. Back row: Jennie Gomersal, Vicky Roch, Hazel Simpson, Michelle Edwards. Front Row: Jo Scott-Smith, Kelly Reay, Karen Morris, Emma Steele. *December 1986* (DSC)

Fig 177. A scrummage in the Dunstablians v Beaconsfield rugby football match.
April 1987 (DG/NW)

Fig 178. 1,000 Scouts marching through Dunstable's High Street North for the St George's Day Service.
April 1987 (DG)

Fig 179. David Stephen (SDP candidate for North Luton), Dr David Owen MP and Nick Hills (SDP candidate for Mid Beds) outside the Chiltern Radio studios in Chiltern Road.
April 1987 (DG)

Fig 180. The rapid introduction of new technology into the classroom has been a feature of the decade. A photograph taken at Northfields Upper School. *May 1987* (NS)

Fig 181. At dawn on Easter Day the Salvation Army leads hymn singing on the Downs, with members of the congregations of the Priory, two Methodist churches, St Fremunds and the New Covenant Church.   *April 1987* (DG)

Fig 182. Extensive improvements to the pavilion at Luton Road Recreation Ground being surveyed by (left) Ron Wiseham (Groundsman) and Ernie Brown (Town Council Works Manager).   *April 1987* (DG)

Fig 183. The Show judge
Graham Lucas (Head Keeper
at Whipsnade Zoo) and
steward Joan Lund look at
one of the pet class entrants at
the annual Cat Show held at
the Queensway Hall.
April 1987 (DG)

Fig 184. David Wilkie the Olympic swimming Gold Medallist joined 400 pupils at Streetfield Middle School in a 1000m jog in the National Sports Aid Run. In the eighties public awareness of Third World needs were greatly heightened, resulting in huge national and international events being organised to try to relieve the effects of drought, famine, war and economic disasters. Bob Geldof (singer with the Boom Town Rats group) organised a hugely successful international television spectacular called "Band Aid" and this was followed by other charitable "Aid" initiatives all through the decade.   *July 1987* (DG)

Fig 185. At the County Swimming Championships in 1987, Jo Scott-Smith and Jennie Gomersal won the Rose Bowl, the Junior Duet trophy, and are pictured holding it. Also in the photograph are the rest of the Dunstable Swimming Club Synchro Section team: front row Jo Scott-Smith, Jennie Gomersal and Emma Steele, middle row Nikki Scott-Smith and Karen Walls, back row Chrissie Allen, Rachael Porter, Lisa Pusey and Dawn Heath. *1987* (DSC)

Fig 186. Christian Holmes, skipper of the Dunstable Dynamos is in the driving seat in this photograph. With him are the rest of the 12–14s team who not only won the Division 2 Championship of the Bovis Chiltern Youth Football League, but were unbeaten throughout. Their manager Gary Roberts holds the cup. *May 1987* (DG)

Fig 187. Falconry is one of the world's oldest sports. In this photograph Ceri Griffiths is coaching a young spectator at Dunstable Carnival.
May 1987 (DG)

Fig 188. An unusual view of the annual Mayormaking in the Queensway Hall. Here Cllr Mrs Wendie Mills makes her acceptance speech. *May 1987* (DG)

Fig 189. July 1987 marked the introduction of the small, fast and frequent Hoppanstopper buses in Dunstable. The design won first prize in a competition at Southampton and soon became a very familiar sight in the town. Here the buses are in The Square. *July 1987* (DG)

◄ Fig 190. The Dunstable and Porz basketball teams playing at Dunstable Park Recreation Centre. *August 1987* (DG)

Fig 191. The Mayor of Dunstable Cllr Mrs Wendie Mills and Cllr Nick Goodman with the new town sign in Luton Road also showing the town's twinning with Porz and Brive. *August 1987* (DG)

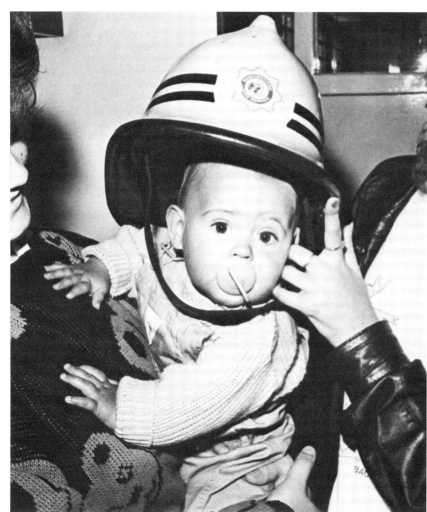

Fig 192. This young visitor is enjoying a visit to the annual Dunstable Fire Station Open Day.
September 1987 (DG/RB)

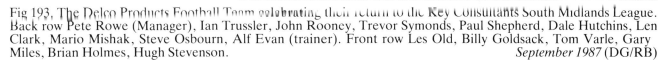

Fig 193. The Delco Products Football Team celebrating their return to the Key Consultants South Midlands League. Back row Pete Rowe (Manager), Ian Trussler, John Rooney, Trevor Symonds, Paul Shepherd, Dale Hutchins, Len Clark, Mario Mishak, Steve Osbourn, Alf Evan (trainer). Front row Les Old, Billy Goldsack, Tom Varle, Gary Miles, Brian Holmes, Hugh Stevenson.
September 1987 (DG/RB)

Fig 194. Dunstable's two deaconesses were ordained as deacons by the Bishop of St Albans, the Right Reverend John Taylor at St John the Baptist Church, Barnet. Liz Hughes from St Augustine's and Stephanie Atkin from The Priory were the first such Dunstable women to join the clergy. They are here photographed with the Venerable Michael Bourke, Archdeacon of Bedford, and are being welcomed as deacons at the Priory Church. *May 1987* (DG/RB)

Fig 195. The 'Dunstabelle' Dunstable to Brighton excursion train arrives at Robinson and White's "station" in Dunstable. It was the first passenger train to leave Dunstable in 22 years. ADAPT (Association for Dunstable Area Passenger Trains) is campaigning to upgrade the local freight line to passenger status once more. *May 1987* (DG/CPA)

Fig 196. Dunstable Women's Institute branch is the oldest in Bedfordshire. The photograph shows the committee at the Dunstable W.I.'s 70th birthday. Seated: Mrs V. Janes, Mrs P. Hardiman, Mrs D. Brazier, Mrs I Wood (Treasurer), Mrs M. Gillbe, Mrs S. Fraser. Standing: Mrs M. Harper, Mrs J. Sharratt, Mrs J. Griffiths (Secretary), Mrs Betty Heritage (President), Mrs P. Gilroy, Mrs B. Storey, Mrs J. Douglas, Mrs S. Eason, Mrs D. Williams.
May 1987 (DWI)

Fig 197. The Houghton Regis and District Flying Club stall at Dunstable Carnival, with John McLoughlin the Club Chairman talking to members of the public.
May 1987 (HRDFC)

Fig 198. The opening of the Tourist Information Centre in Dunstable Library by Mrs Fielding (President of the Thames and Chiltern Tourist Board). Also in the photograph are Helena Kuzycz (2nd left, who ran the Centre), Cllr J. Pergunas (Chairman, South Beds District Council), Cllr J.P.B. Kinchella (Chairman, Beds County Council) and Cllr Mrs Wendie Mills (Town Mayor). *July 1987* (DG/RB)

Fig 199. High Street North crossing High Street South! A large photographic print of the old High Street North being delivered by Andrew Hickman of Chiltern Photographic Arts (right) and Justin Tearle. The photograph was specially commissioned for the opening of Herington's new pharmacy in Ashton Square. Heringtons celebrated their 100th anniversary in the town in July. *June 1987* (DG/CPA)

Fig 200. This unusually shaped tree was known as the "H" tree and grew at the rear of 52 High Street South. This photograph is taken from behind the tree and, looking through the open doors of the wide entrance way, can be seen High Street South. The tree was cut down for the Friary site development. *1987* (BE)

Fig 201. The straw hat factory buildings at the rear of 52 High Street South before the Friary site development. *1987* (UB)

Fig 202. The Priory Engraving building was a 19th century bakery. To the left is the small 19th century hat factory building at the rear of the Grey House in High Street South. *1987* (DTC/LE)

Fig 203. The Band Concerts organised by the Town Council in Priory Gardens on Sunday afternoons proved very popular. *June 1987* (DTC/CPA)

Fig 200.

Fig 201.

Fig 202.

Fig 203.

Fig 204. An aerial view of Dunstable College with the Magistrates Court in the left hand foreground and the Ambulance Station middle foreground.   1988 (DTC)

Fig 205. Dunstable Market moved to a new home in March 1988. It had been on the site shown in the background of this photograph, between Court Drive and the Library, for nearly 25 years. Previous to that it had been held in High Street North from the crossroads to Albion Street. The new site is shown in the foreground on the north-west side of the Queensway Hall. It is called the Queensway Market Square. *March 1988* (DG/RB)

Fig 206. The Market on its new site. *March 1988* (DTC/MP)

101

Fig 207. The scene in Dunstable Telephone Exchange when a £12.5m modernisation programme was brought into use. *March 1988* (DG)

Fig 208. Robin Ellis is shown in Dunstable Library talking about his life as an actor and his leading role in the television series "Poldark". His book on the making of the series is in the foreground.
April 1988 (DG/RB)

April 1988 (DG)

Fig 209. Dunstable Amateur Operatic Society's production of Half a Sixpence.

Fig 210. Red clown noses were sold nationwide for charity. Here Dyno-Rod workers Geoff Fearan, Arthur Sarisa and Garry Johnson are supporting the Comic Relief Red Nose Day.
February 1988 (DG/DR)

Fig 211. Town Mayor Cllr Mrs Wendie Mills organised a May Day Youth Fayre on Priory Meadow, when all the Town's youth organisations put on exhibitions and displays. Here she is pictured taking a ride on a gun carriage pulled by Dunstable Sea Cadets.
May 1988 (DG/RB)

1988

Fig 212. In Church Street, under the railway bridge, firemen plunged into flood water to rescue this car driver.
July 1988 (DG/RW)

Fig 213. The high wire act at Dunstable Carnival thrills the crowd.   *May 1988* (RW)

Fig 214. Fire over England celebrations. Town Council staff erecting a replica Elizabethan Beacon on Dunstable Downs. A chain of beacons were lit across the country on 19th July 1988 to celebrate the 400th Anniversary of the sighting of the Spanish Armada. Over 45,000 people attended this, the largest event ever held in the town.   *July 1988* (CPA)

Fig 215. Deputy Mayor Ken Biswell and County Council Chairman John Kinchella light the Dunstable Beacon after receiving the signal from Windsor Great Park. From the Downs the national chain of beacons split westwards to Muswell Hill, Oxon, and northwards to Althorp Park, Northants.   *July 1988* (RW)

Fig 216. Dozens of local charities manned stalls and provided entertainment in period dress at the celebrations. In the foreground are members of the Dunstable Branch of RNLI. In the background is Dunstable Round Table's Ox Roast. The ox took 24 hours to roast over a coal coke and wood fire, and provided 1,600–1,700 portions.
July 1988 (DTC/CPA)

Fig 217. To celebrate the golden jubilee of the Women's Royal Voluntary Service Sheila Kitchen, the District Organiser, "plants" a commemorative plaque in a flowerbed in Priory Gardens. Helping Mrs Kitchen is Mrs Dorothy Ward (County Organiser) and Mr Ernie Brown (Works Manager for Dunstable Town Council). The flowerbed was donated by Dunstable Town Council to the Dunstable and District WRVS for their jubilee, and Mrs Kitchen's husband Don made the plaque for the occasion.   *July 1988* (WRVS)

Fig 218. The New Covenant Church in West Street is in the background of this photograph. In July 1988 the Church organised the Chiltern Christian Festival which was held in a large marquee near the Dunstable Park Recreation Centre. The photograph shows the beginning of the "Make Way" march through the town to the marquee.   *July 1988* (NCC)

Fig 219. On his retirement, Sam Caen (Development and Works Executive, South Beds District Council) is pictured in front of one of his projects – the design and construction of Dunstable Park Recreation Centre. The new South Beds District Council's offices in High Street North, opened in 1989, were also one of Mr Caen's projects. Mr Caen had been in local government for 43 years, coming to Dunstable in 1968 as the borough engineer and surveyor of Dunstable Borough Council. *June 1988* (DG/JS)

Fig 220. Dunstable bookseller and publisher Paul Bowes scored a hat-trick when he published books by three local authors on the same day. The books were Old Houghton by Pat Lovering (left), Local Walks: South Bedfordshire and North Chilterns by Vaughan Basham and John Bunyan: His Life and Times by Vivienne Evans. They were published under Paul's imprint of The Book Castle. The photograph was taken at the books' launch in Dunstable Library. *July 1988* (RB)

Fig 221. The Quadrant shopping precinct was built in the sixties and extensively modernised in 1987. This view is looking down Broad Walk towards Vernon Place.
1988 (DTC)

Fig 222. A scene from the Junior Rep's production of A Midsummer Night's Dream. In the back row left to right are: Antoinette Scales, Natasha Mullany, Adrian Cooper, Craig McCahill and in the front: Gareth Baker and Gregor McBraine.
June 1988 (TDRTC/NW)

Fig 223. The first-ever Dunstable Arts Festival was highly successful. It included forty-two events in sixteen days. Here the Town Mayor Brenda Boatwright is purchasing the first Arts Festival tickets at the opening of the Festival Box Office in Dunstable Library on 15th August 1988. She is accompanied by members of the Arts Festival Committee, from left to right: Ted Anketell-Jones (Official Announcer), Cllr Nicholas Goodman (Chairman), Helen Ayres (Town Council Community Development Officer), the Town Mayor, Richard Walden (Town Clerk), John Darby (Technical Adviser), Paul Bowes (Rotary Club of Dunstable), Alison Harding (Hon Secretary).   *August 1988* (DTC/BT)

Fig 224. The Civic and Festival Service was at the Priory Church of St Peter on October 9th 1988. The photograph shows the Town Mayor Cllr Mrs Brenda Boatwright with Mr Peter Boatwright (right) and Macebearer Roy Wilson, flanked by standard bearers of some of the Town's uniformed organisations.   *October 1988* (DTC/BT)

Fig 225. The renowned actress Miss Prunella Scales outside the Queensway Hall on 2nd October 1988 prior to her performance of An Evening with Queen Victoria, part of the Arts Festival programme. With her are Ian Partridge (tenor) and Christopher Kite (piano).   *October 1988* (DTC/BT)

Fig 226. One of the highlights of the Arts Festival was the Literary Dinner on October 6th at the Queensway Hall. Dinner was served to an accompaniment by members of Dunstable Music School and then three popular modern authors gave witty and well received after-dinner speeches. The photograph shows the authors signing copies of their recently-published books: Mel Calman with Modern Times, Gerald Priestland with The Unquiet Suitcase and John Seymour with England Revisited.   *October 1988* (DTC/JC)

Fig 227. The Arts Festival Schools Showcase took place in the Queensway Hall on the 13th October 1988. This is part of the huge audience showing in the front row Fred Moore (Chief Steward), Town Mayor Cllr Mrs Brenda Boatwright and Cllr Mrs Joan Goodall.   *October 1988* (DTC/BT)

Fig 228. Another photograph of the Schools Showcase showing part of the Lower Schools Choir, with pupils from Watling Lower School in the foreground.   *October 1988* (DTC/BT)

Fig 229. The Arts Festival Orchestral Concert in St Mary's Roman Catholic Church on 15th October 1988. A packed audience enjoys the performance by the Serenata of London. In the front row are (left) Cllr Peter Rawcliffe (Chairman, South Beds District Council), Mrs Pat Cross, Peter Boatwright and Cllr Mrs Brenda Boatwright (Town Mayor).   *October 1988* (DTC/BT)

Fig 230. Another view of the Arts Festival Orchestral Concert in St Mary's Church, showing the Serenata of London, leader Barry Wilde (front left).   *October 1988* (DTC/BT)

Fig 231. A wall sign showing the sign of the Guild of Carpenters, refurbished and replaced on what was recorded as a public house in the 19th century. The house is number 116/118 in High Street South.   *June 1988* (DG/RB)

Fig 232. Moore's in High Street South celebrated its eightieth anniversary in November 1988. The photograph shows Pauline Keen (President of the Dunstable Chamber of Commerce in 1989) and her father Fred Moore standing in the shop. The shop is in an eighteenth century listed building, and was originally two shops both occupied at various times in the 19th century by members of the Tibbett family, Dunstable's 19th century printers and publishers. It was Daniel Tibbett who founded the Dunstable Borough Gazette in 1865. Charles F. Moore moved into number 21 High Street South in 1917 and took over number 23 when Boots the Chemists moved to the Quadrant.   *November 1988* (M/MP)

Fig 233. R.H. Bunker's butcher's shop on the corner of Union Street and Edward Street before its redevelopment as Bunker's Court. *1988* (BE)

Fig. 234. The Old Sugar Loaf, a Berni Inn refurbished in July 1985, in High Street North. It was built in c.1717 and was a famous and luxurious coaching inn, once visited by Queen Victoria. *1988* (DTC)

Fig 235. The hundredth anniversary of the founding of Dunstable Grammar School was celebrated in September 1988. It had been founded with funds from the estate of Frances Ashton, a member of one of Dunstable's important charitable families. In July 1971 following the reorganisation of local schools, staff and pupils moved into a new purpose-built comprehensive school on the present Manshead Upper School campus. The Headmaster at this time was Mr L.P. Banfield (Headmaster 1960–1980). Mr D. Beacham was appointed head of Ashton Middle School as the building then became. In the photograph is a former Deputy Head and former Mayor of Dunstable Mr W.T. Lack OBE, who taught at the school from 1924 to 1964.

September 1988 (DG/JS)

Fig 236. This photograph was taken outside the main entrance of the school during the hundredth anniversary celebrations and shows a group of some of those present at the school in the thirties. The building is now Ashton Middle School.   *September 1988* (CEB/JS)

Fig 237. Over 1,000 people visited the Manshead Archaeological Society's dig on the site of the Friary, before redevelopment took place. At this site carved masonry, stained glass, coins and glazed tiles were found from periods over the last 600 years, together with the skeleton of a horse in a Roman well! *September 1988* (DG/RB)

Fig 238. The last of the town's red telephone boxes being removed, to be replaced by the new metallic grey ones. *December 1988* (DG/CPA)

1989

Fig 239. Garry Richards (left) and Garry Acoursini changed a set of wheels in 96.49 seconds at Silverstone in a National Tyre Distributors Association Fast Fitter of the Year competition. The advertisement for unleaded petrol in the background of this photograph reflects the increasing public concern with pollution and the environment which was so noticeable in the latter part of the eighties. *January 1989* (DG)

Fig 240. Beverly Hughes, owner and trainer, from the Dunstable and District Dog Training Club with Woughstock Wisdom her seven year old Border Collie. Woughstock Wisdom was Cruft's Obedience Supreme Champion and is seen here with his rosettes and certificates. *February 1989* (DG)

Figs 241, 242 and 243. Three new stained glass windows installed in the South Aisle of the Priory, designed by John Hayward. This is one of five sets of windows, four of them designed by John Hayward and the other by Christopher Webb, all given by Mr and Mrs T.C. Flory as a memorial to their son who died in the nineteen sixties. The set in the photographs shows scenes from the life of St Peter: Fig 241 shows his calling, Fig 242 his frailty in the Garden of Gethsemane and Fig 243 Christ's charge to St Peter, "Feed my lambs, feed my sheep." *January 1989* (DG/MP)

Fig 244. Les Matthews was made a Fellow of the Royal Society of Antiquarians in 1985. He started local digs in 1937 with fellow enthusiasts and in 1953 founded the Manshead Archaeological Society and was subsequently involved in many important local excavations. Dunstable can be proud of its rich history, so much of which Les Matthews helped to illuminate. He died in February 1989 and a revised edition of his book "Ancient Dunstable" (originally published 1963) was published by the Manshead Archaeological Society in November 1989. *undated* (JSc)

Fig 245. Phillip Thigay (left) and Martin Taylor practising for the Junior 4-man Canoe Team World Championships in Canada. Both are students at Queensbury Upper School. *March 1989* (DG/RB)

119

Fig 246. Local Guides at the Thinking Day Service at the Methodist Church, celebrating the centenary of the birth of former World Chief Guide Lady Olave Baden-Powell.
March 1989 (DG/RB)

Fig 247. The area's first Rainbow Guides in the congregation at the Thinking Day Service at the Methodist Church. The Rainbow Guides group is aimed at those girls not old enough to be a Brownie Guide.   (DG/RB)

Fig 248. The choristers at the Priory "walk and sing" round local churches to raise funds for the Church Urban Fund. The 25 choristers were accompanied by their family and friends and walked to (and sang at) St Fremund's – Eaton Bray – Totternhoe – St Mary's Catholic Church and back to the Priory. Here they are just setting out.

March 1989 (DG/RB)

Fig 249. Members of the Dunstable and District Handicapped Persons Typing Club at their 21st anniversary service with the Mayor of Dunstable Cllr Mrs Brenda Boatwright. *April 1989* (DG/RB)

Fig 250. The Dunstable College Music Society is shown here tuning up for their "Spring in the Air" concert. The Society includes a mixed choir and an orchestra.
April 1989 (DG/JC)

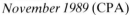

Fig 251. The Peter Newton Pavilion is dedicated to the late Peter Newton JP, twice mayor of Dunstable and was opened to the public in May. The building and grounds were refurbished with the help of Tesco stores and provide for all sections of the community with its many activities and extensive indoor and outdoor facilities. It incorporates six acres of public open space. The Tesco store, part of which can be seen in the centre background, opened in October. The site had formerly been the Laporte Sports Ground.
November 1989 (CPA)

Fig 252. Marching along High Street North, the 5th Dunstable Apache Cub Pack and its Leader Roger Cladd head the St George's Day Parade to the service at St Mary's Catholic Church in West Street.
April 1989 (DG/RB)

Fig 253. The Ascot Scene from the Dunstable Amateur Operatic Society's production of "My Fair Lady". The DAOS was formed at a meeting at Ashton Primary School on May 5th 1964 and celebrated its 25th anniversary this year. *April 1989* (DAOS)

Fig 254. In September Queensbury Upper School became the first school in the county to be grant maintained. Here David Madel MP is holding the key of the door ready to open the school building, watched by chairman of governors Peter Roberts (left), headmaster Dr Keith Barker (centre) and pupils.
September 1989 (DG/JS)

Fig 225 Maurice Manning, (District Manager for Post Office Counters), Cllr Mrs Brenda Boatwright (Mayor of Dunstable) and Peter Rawcliffe (Chairman of South Bedfordshire District Council) opening the refurbished Post Office in High Street North.
May 1989 (DG)

Fig 256. Dunstable's Periwinkle Lane water borehole had been contaminated with trichloroethylene (used for dry cleaning or cleaning diesel engines) since 1985. There had also been worries about high levels of nitrates in drinking water, reflecting a concern with pollution of all kinds which became a theme throughout the country in the late eighties. The photograph shows town and district councillors visiting the new treatment plant at Beech Road as it was about to be commissioned. The new plant is designed to reduce the offending contamination in local water supplies.
July 1989 (DG/MP)

Fig 257. The Town Council meeting at The Friars, High Street South. The photograph shows from left to right: Councillors Terry Matcham, Paul Barter, Nicholas Goodman, Tony Jackson, Town Clerk Richard Walden, Town Mayor Brenda Boatwright, Ken Biswell, Wendie Mills, Mike Tilley, Joan Goodall and Doreen MacLachlan. *1989* (DTC)

Fig 258. The new South Bedfordshire District Council offices in the course of construction. *1989* (VB)

Fig 259. The Carnival Procession led by the Luton Royal British Legion Pipes and Drums.
May 1989 (DG/RB)

Fig 260. Another feature of the eighties was the number of large-scale disasters: not only natural disasters like the great storms of 1987, but man-made ones like the sinking of the Herald of Free Enterprise, the fire at the Bradford football ground, the Kings Cross fire and the crushing of football fans at the Hillsborough football ground in April 1989. Here the Dunstablians Rugby Club players and a team from the Saracens Head observe a silence before their charity match in aid of the Hillsborough Disaster Fund. *May 1989* (DG/RB)

Fig 261. The fourth year walking and hostelling club at Priory Middle School won the Tanners Marathon Association trophy for the third year running. To mark this unique achievement Alan Virgo, a representative of the Association, came to the school to present the trophy in person. With him in the photograph are Martin Bacon and Steve Bowles, the first two to complete the course. All thirteen walkers finished.
July 1989 (DG/JS)

Fig 262. Dr Sam Twivy retired after 38 years as a Dunstable GP. He is pictured in his garden in Eaton Bray.
July 1989 (DG/JS)

Fig 263. The launch of one of a series of town information leaflets produced by the Town Council at the "Day Out in Thames and Chilterns" Exhibition at the Queensway Hall in February 1989. Pictured are Cllr Nicholas Goodman (Chairman of the Town Council's Tourism Committee), Stan Bowes (Marketing Director, Thames and Chilterns Tourist Board), Helen Ayres (Town Council Community Officer), Cllr Mrs Brenda Boatwright (Mayor of Dunstable) and Christopher Jennings (Director of the Tourist Board).
February 1989 (DTC/RB)

Fig 264. The mural on the south east wall of the Queensway Hall is a stylised representation of an aerial view of the buildings around the crossroads.
August 1989 (PL)

Fig 265. A view of the crossroads looking west from Quadrant House.
August 1989 (PL)

Fig 266. Looking north from Quadrant House towards the tower of All Saints Houghton Regis in the background. In the middle foreground is the Magistrates Court and Ambulance Station and behind that and to the right, Dunstable College.
August 1989 (PL)

Fig 267. The annual orange-rolling ceremony at Lancot Lower School has taken place for about 20 years and is preceded by country dancing. Oranges are rolled down the Lancot Mounds (the earth mounds on the school field) and the children catch them. The ceremony is a revival of a local tradition of orange rolling from Pascomb Pit on Dunstable Downs on Good Friday. *May 1989* (DG/JS)

Fig 268. The Marchioness of Tavistock at Dunstable Police Station opening the victim support suite. On the left is Chief Superintendent Brian Prickett and on the right the Mayor of Dunstable, Cllr Ken Biswell. *August 1989* (DG/RB)

Fig 269. In 1981, the independent Pilgrim Christian School opened as a ministry of the New Covenant Church, meeting the needs of parents who wanted their children's education to be set in a framework of Christian belief. The children work in the buildings of the West Street Christian Centre and the photograph shows pupils studying the ecology of chalkland on Dunstable Downs.   *1989* (NCC)

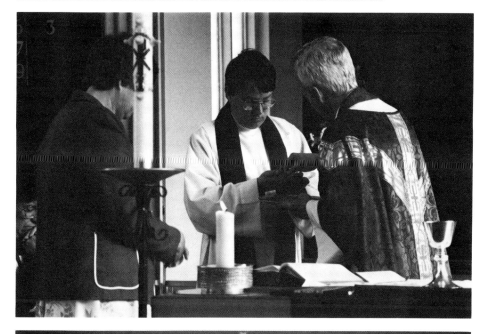

Fig 270. The Rev Paul Hughes, Team Vicar at St Augustine's, is receiving Holy Communion from the Rector, the Rev David Self. The chappatis, which replaced communion wafers at this special service, were made by Luton children whose backgrounds represent six different countries. The children are taught by a parishioner at St Augustine's.
                    May 1989 (DS)

Fig 271. A farewell party in Chew's House for Peter Stokes, the Priory choirmaster for the past two years. The cake, specially made by Ann Bowes, included small models of members of the choir. The originals of the models are standing round in anticipation as Peter cuts the cake.
          September 1989 (DG/MP)

Fig 272. The purpose built South Bedfordshire District Council offices in High Street North. The offices were built at a cost of over six million pounds and house 400 staff who were previously based at Dunstable, Houghton Regis and Leighton Buzzard. *September 1989* (SBDC/BT)

Fig 273. The Duke of Gloucester carried out the opening ceremony in September and is here photographed sheltering under Chairman of the SBDC Cllr Mrs Beesley's umbrella, held by the chairman's officer Roy Wilson. In the background are Cllr Peter Roberts (Vice Chairman of the District Council), Cllr Mrs Angela Roberts, Cllr Harold Heath, Cllr Bert Whinnett and Mrs Heath. *September 1989* (SBDC/MP)

Fig 274. Grove House, in High Street North, was built as an inn in the 18th century. It was bought by the local council in the thirties and turned into Municipal Offices. It housed offices of the South Bedfordshire District Council until their move to new premises in September 1989. The building itself was then refurbished as far as possible in line with a private dwelling of the thirties and used to house the offices of Dunstable Town Council. *1988* (VB)

Fig 275. The Ladies Lodge Almshouses in Church Street, built c 1743 to provide homes for "six maiden gentlewomen" by two local sisters Blandina Marshe and Mary Lockington. Another example of a long tradition of charitable giving in the town, they both made generous provision in their wills to help the poor. *undated* (DTC/AH)

Fig 276. The Christmas lights in High Street North brighten up the wintry street. *January 1989* (DG)

Index
(by page number)

Fig 277. The Quadrant in 1980, before its facelift.   *January 1980* (CPA)

Fig 278. Two vital aspects of Dunstable's well-being –
cleaning the town's streets of litter . . .   *1988* (UB)

Fig 279. . . . and clearing up after the Saturday Market.
                                August 1989 (PL)

Mayors and Deputy Mayors of Dunstable
1979 – 1990

Year	Mayor	Deputy Mayor
1979/80	Cllr C.G. Clark	Cllr W. Allen
1980/81	Cllr W. Allen	Cllr P.J. Newton
1981/82	Cllr P.J. Newton	Cllr T.W.R. Bamford
1982/83	Cllr S.C. Brett	Cllr J.R. McAllister
1983/84	Cllr J.R. McAllister	Cllr W. Allen
1984/85	Cllr W. Allen	Cllr T.W.R. Bamford
1985/86	Cllr N.P. Goodman	Cllr A.A.B. Musannif
1986/87	Cllr A.A.B. Musannif	Cllr Mrs W.A. Mills
1987/88	Cllr Mrs W.A. Mills	Cllr G. Davies
1988/89	Cllr Mrs B.M. Boatwright	Cllr K.S. Biswell
1989/90	Cllr K.S. Biswell	Cllr M. Tilley

Town Clerks

1975 – 1985   Mrs Ina Rosie, Clerk to the Charter Trustees and Secretary to the Town Mayor.

1985 – present   Mr Richard Walden, Town Clerk.

Key to Sources of Photographs and Photographers

(by figure numbers)

Fig 280. A detail from the otherwise unremarkable frontage of the Coral Social Club Ltd's Bingo Hall (formerly the town's cinema) in High Street North.

August 1989 (PL)

Books Published by
THE BOOK CASTLE

NORTH CHILTERNS CAMERA, 1863–1954; FROM THE THURSTON COLLECTION IN LUTON MUSEUM: edited by Stephen Bunker
Rural landscapes, town views, studio pictures and unique royal portraits by the area's leading early photographer.

JOURNEYS INTO BEDFORDSHIRE: Anthony Mackay
Foreword by The Marquess of Tavistock.
A lavish book of over 150 evocative ink drawings.

FOLK: CHARACTERS and EVENTS in the HISTORY OF BEDFORDSHIRE and NORTHAMPTONSHIRE: Vivienne Evans
Arranged by village/town, an anthology of stories about the counties' most intriguing historical figures.

ECHOES: TALES and LEGENDS of BEDFORDSHIRE and HERTFORDSHIRE: Vic Lea
Thirty, compulsively retold historical incidents.

TERESA of WATLING STREET: Arnold Bennett
Introduced by Simon Houfe.
The only detective story by one of the twentieth century's most famous novelists. Written and set in Bedfordshire.

A LASTING IMPRESSION: Michael Dundrow
An East End boy's wartime experiences as an evacuee on a Chilterns farm at Totternhoe.

JOHN BUNYAN: HIS LIFE and TIMES: Vivienne Evans
Foreword by the Bishop of Bedford.
Bedfordshire's most famous son set in his seventeenth century context.

LOCAL WALKS: SOUTH BEDFORDSHIRE and NORTH CHILTERNS: Vaughan Basham
Twenty seven thematic circular walks.

DUNSTABLE IN DETAIL: Nigel Benson
A hundred of the town's buildings and features, past and present, plus town-trail map.

OLD DUNSTABLE: Bill Twaddle
A new edition of this collection of early photographs.

ROYAL HOUGHTON: Pat Lovering
Illustrated history of Houghton Regis from earliest times to the present day.

OLD HOUGHTON, INCLUDING UPPER HOUGHTON, NOW PART OF DUNSTABLE: Pat Lovering
Over 170 photographs of Houghton Regis during the last 100 years.

Further titles are in preparation.

All the above are available via any bookshop,
or from the publisher and bookseller
THE BOOK CASTLE,
12 Church Street, Dunstable, Bedfordshire LU5 4RU. Tel (0582) 605670